T0198810

I'M PRETTY, TOO:
Embracing differences

NAOMI CONNOR

ILLUSTRATIONS BY:
IRENE OLDS

AuthorHouse™
1663 Liberty Drive
Bloomington, IN 47403
www.authorhouse.com
Phone: 833-262-8899

This book is printed on acid-free paper.

ISBN: 978-1-4772-8384-4 (sc)
978-1-4817-0273-7 (e)

Library of Congress Control Number: 2012920125

Print information available on the last page.

Published by AuthorHouse 02/25/2021

authorHOUSE®

This book focuses on building inner strength. For a child, any child, growing up with the positives; confidence, assurance, safety, endurance are cornerstones to their development. These are but a few of the many traits needed as a foundation on their journey to maturity.

Naomi Connor

My eyes are hazel, blue, brown or green

No matter the color, the purpose is to see!

I'M PRETTY, TOO

I have a genuine smile that opens many doors.

Whatever its focus, it brightens the soul.

I'M PRETTY, TOO

If standing quite tall and barely a sliver

Or short and plump with a robust figure.

I'M PRETTY, TOO

My skin is golden with variations of light

By origins of birth or from the effects of sunlight.

I'M PRETTY, TOO

Having hair that is curly, thick and soft like wool

Or fine and straight like thread on a spool!

I'M PRETTY, TOO

13

Sometimes by accident or maybe by fate

Things don't work out as planned.

The parts don't work like originally made

But can be repaired on demand.

The word "pretty" is subjective. It's not what I aspire to be.

The words "learning" and "learned" have more meaning to me.

To seek and use knowledge with courage to do my best

Is nothing less than "beautiful" and puts "pretty" to the test.

So I revel in who I am and the person that I will grow up to be

'Cause pretty is as pretty does looking at it subjectively.

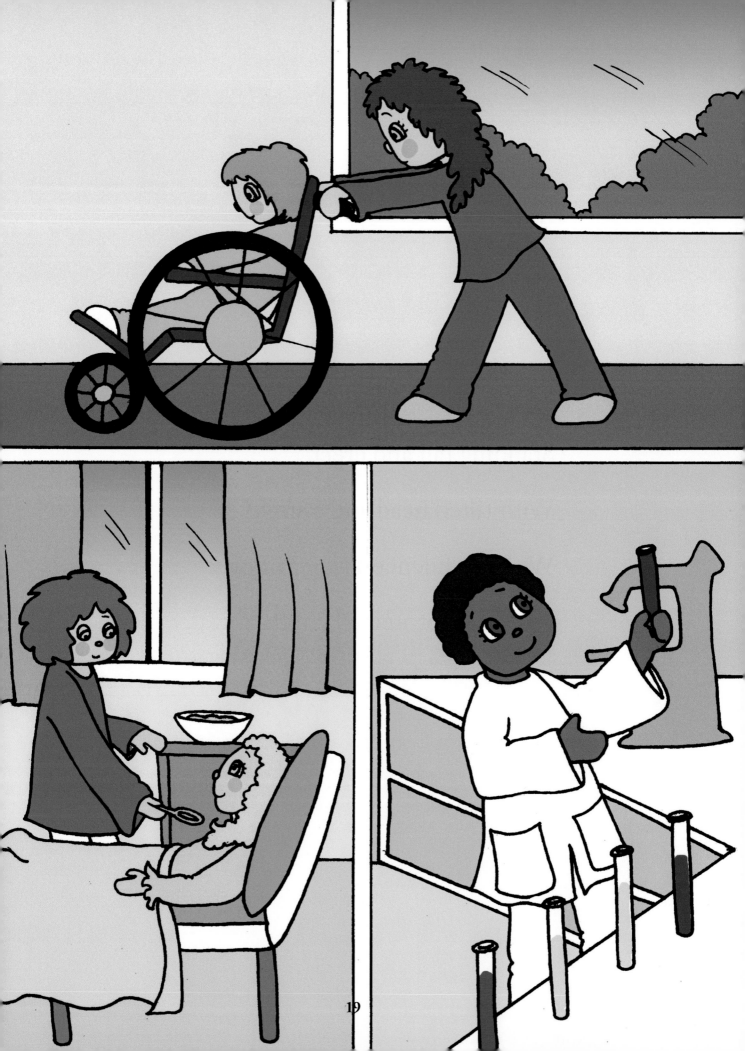

Standing tall and erect

With tilted head and a smile

With confidence as my armor,

I'm a well-protected child.

So as I stand in front of the mirror

Observing a face that is familiar to me

Looking beyond the mere physical

I like what I see!

But most of all.......

I'm pretty just being me !!!!!!!!!!!

Printed in the United States
by Baker & Taylor Publisher Services